Points: 0.5

4284
Looking at Faces in Art

Joy Richardson
AR B.L.: 3.0 POINTS: 0.5
Points: 0.5

W9-AOY-165

DATE DUE

450076   Looking at faces in art

HOW TO LOOK AT ART

Looking at Faces *in art*

Joy Richardson

Gareth Stevens Publishing
MILWAUKEE

For a free color catalog describing Gareth Stevens' list of high-quality books and multimedia programs, call 1-800-542-2595 (USA) or 1-800-461-9120 (Canada). Gareth Stevens Publishing's Fax: (414) 225-0377.

Gareth Stevens Publishing would like to thank Gundega Spons of the Milwaukee Art Museum for her kind and professional help with the information in this book.

Library of Congress Cataloging-in-Publication Data available upon request from publisher.
Fax (414) 225-0377 for the attention of the Publishing Records Department.

ISBN 0-8368-2624-8

This North American edition first published in 2000 by
Gareth Stevens Publishing
1555 North RiverCenter Drive, Suite 201
Milwaukee, Wisconsin 53212 USA

Original edition © 1997 by Franklin Watts. First published in 1997 as *Making Faces* by Franklin Watts, 96 Leonard Street, London, EC2A 4RH, United Kingdom. This U.S. edition © 2000 by Gareth Stevens, Inc. Additional end matter © 2000 by Gareth Stevens, Inc.

Gareth Stevens Editor: Monica Rausch
Gareth Stevens Cover Designer: Joel Bucaro
U.K. Editor: Sarah Ridley
U.K. Art Director: Robert Walster
U.K. Designer: Louise Thomas

Photographs: Copyright British Museum/Reg. no. 13595 pp. 4-5, 30 (detail); copyright photo RMN/L'ete/ Archimboldo pp. 10-11, RMN/The Cheat Holding the Ace of Diamonds/La Tour pp. 14-15, 28 (detail), RMN/Doctor Paul Gachet/van Gogh pp. 22-23; reproduced by courtesy of the Trustees, National Gallery, London, Ghirlandaio/Portrait of a Girl pp. 6-7, 27 (detail); Cranach/Portraits of Johann the Steadfast and Johann Friedrich the Magnanimous pp. 8-9; Champaigne/Triple Portrait of Cardinal Richelieu pp. 12-13, 27 (detail), 29 (detail); Chardin/The Young Schoolmistress pp. 16-17; Hogarth/The Graham Children cover, pp. 18-19, 28 (detail); Le Brun/Self-Portrait in a Straw Hat pp. 20-21, 31 (detail); Succession Picasso/DACS 1997 Weeping Woman, Pablo Picasso/copyright Tate Gallery, London, pp. 24-25.

Printed in Mexico

1 2 3 4 5 6 7 8 9 04 03 02 01 00

Contents

For additional information about the artists and paintings, see pages 30-31.

Portrait on a Roman Mummy

painted by an unknown artist

This face of a boy who lived in Roman times was painted on wood and preserved with his mummy.

He has a wide, round forehead and a pointed chin.

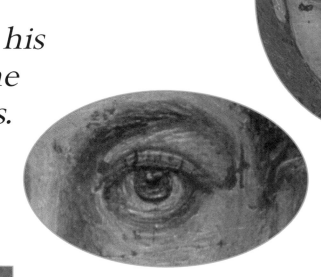

Light glints in his eye beneath the spiky eyelashes.

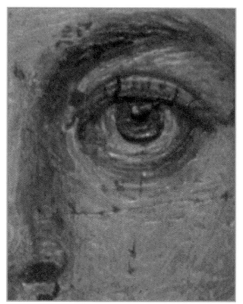

Arched eyebrows lead down to his nose.

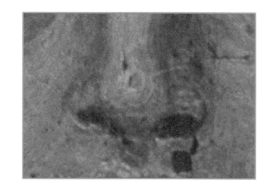

Dark dabs form the nostrils.

Portrait of a Girl
painted by Ghirlandaio

This girl lived five hundred years ago.
The painting captures her image forever.

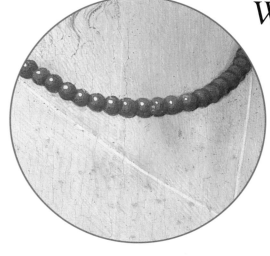

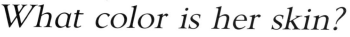
What color is her skin?

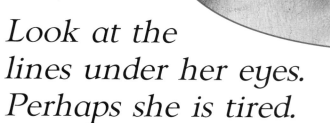

Look at the
lines under her eyes.
Perhaps she is tired.

Is she smiling?

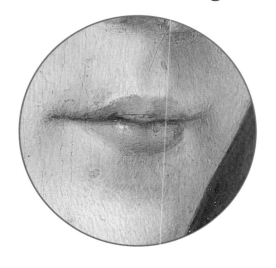

Can you see the light
shining on her hair?

Johann the Steadfast and Johann Friedrich the Magnanimous

painted by Lucas Cranach

The man was an important ruler. His six-year-old son looks grand in his best clothes.

Do you think the boy looks like his father?

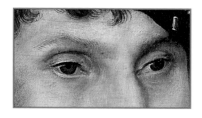 Look how
these eyes look older
than these eyes.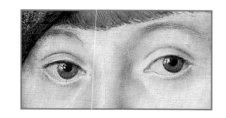

The boy's face is
framed by golden
hair and a very
fine hat.

Whose noses are these?

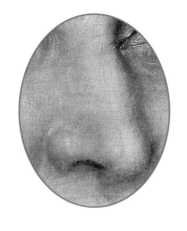 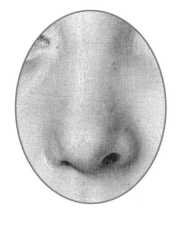

Look how the
shading makes the
noses stand out.

Summer

painted by Giuseppe Archimboldo

The artist painted Summer as
a face full of fruits and vegetables.

The peas in a pod are Summer's
teeth. Look for the cherry lips.

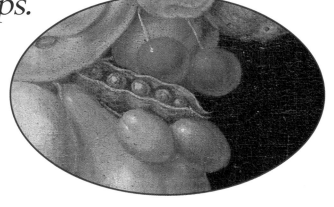

Find the eye, the eyelids,
and the eyebrow.

The peach
acts as a
bulging cheek.

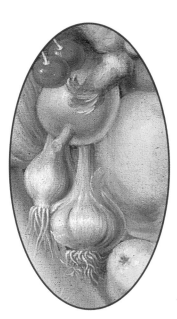

What parts of the
face are these?

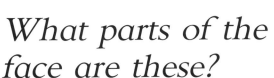

Triple Portrait of Cardinal Richelieu

painted by Philippe de Champaigne

The painter shows the same man from the front and from each side, all in the same picture.

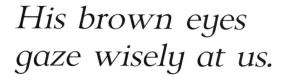

His brown eyes
gaze wisely at us.

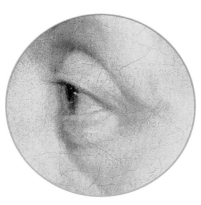

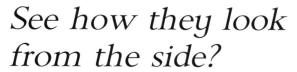

See how they look
from the side?

Look at his tidy mustache
and his shaved skin.

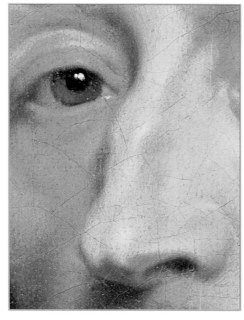

He has a bump on his nose.
Can you see it in the side views?

Are both sides of his face exactly the same?

The Cheat with the Ace of Diamonds

painted by Georges de La Tour

Someone is cheating and has cards behind his back.
Do the others know what is going on?

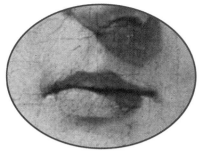

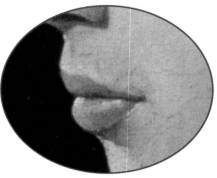

No one is saying anything.
Look at all the closed mouths.

Look at the shape of the
faces. This face is oval, like
an egg. Follow her eyes.
At what are they looking?

Light and shadows
fall on the faces.
From where is the
light coming?

The Young Schoolmistress
painted by Jean-Baptiste-Siméon Chardin

The older girl points to the letters.
The young child is trying to read.

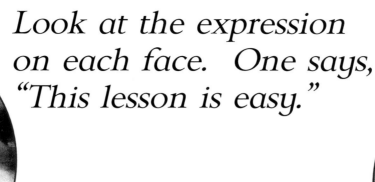

Look at the expression
on each face. One says,
"This lesson is easy."

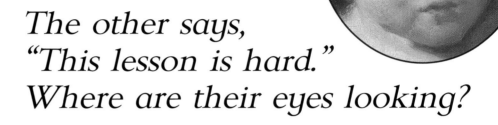

The other says,
"This lesson is hard."
Where are their eyes looking?

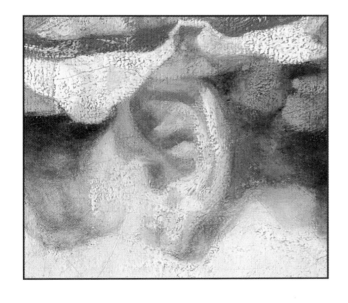

The older girl's face
is shown from the
side. We can see
her entire ear.

Can you find these
colors in their cheeks?

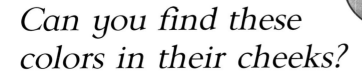

The Graham Children
painted by William Hogarth

This portrait shows the children in their best clothes. Can you see the family likeness?

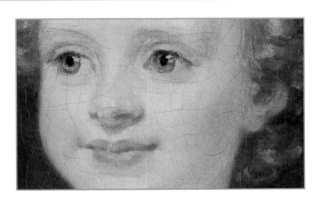

Each face is turned slightly.
How many ears can you see?

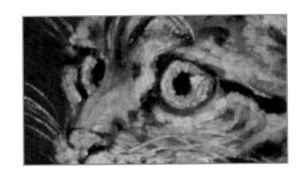

Look at
the shapes
of the faces.
Are they alike?

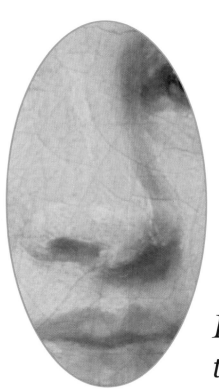

How are the noses painted
to make them stand out?

At what are
these eyes
looking?

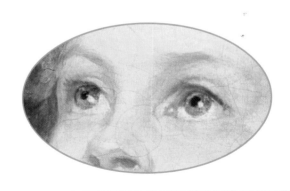

Self-Portrait in a Straw Hat
painted by Élisabeth Marie-Louise Vigée Le Brun

This is a self-portrait. The painter must have looked closely at herself in a mirror.

Look at the colors on her palette.

Which colors does
she use for . . .

her hair?

her eyes?

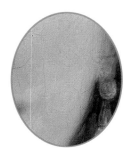

her skin?

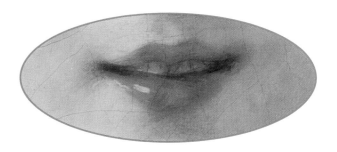

her mouth?

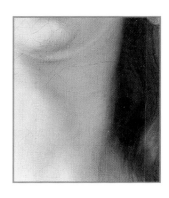

How does she
make the shadows
on her skin?

Doctor Paul Gachet
painted by Vincent van Gogh

Van Gogh painted his friend, the doctor.
Van Gogh knew his friend well.

Look at the pale blue eyes.

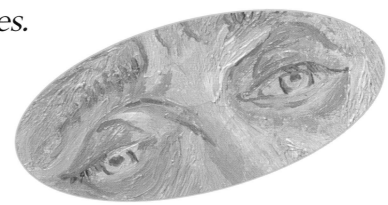

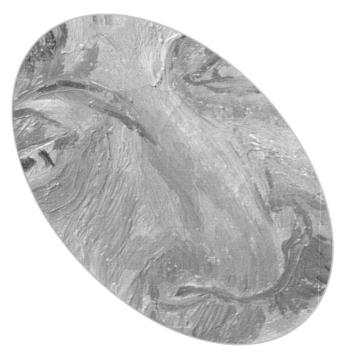

Follow the long nose
down to the thin lips.

He has a thoughtful look, with
knuckles pressed into his cheek.

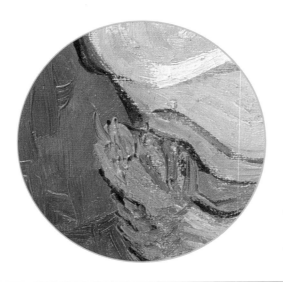

Black lines frame
his cap and bushy hair.

Weeping Woman
painted by Pablo Picasso

This woman has stylish hair
and a fancy hat, but she feels very sad.

Can you see startled eyebrows,

tears coming out
of her eyes,

jagged lines around
her crying mouth,

and fingers gripping
a handkerchief?

The colors also show her feelings.
Look at the cold white, the sour
yellow, and all the thick, black lines.

Making Faces

Skin colors

Skin is not just one color, such as white, brown, or red. Skin is a mixture of colors. Different parts of the body may be slightly different in color.

Try mixing paint to match the color of your skin.

For help, look back at pages 6, 12, 16, and 20.

Painting hair

It would be impossible to paint every strand of hair on a subject's head. Try using brush strokes to show straight hair, curly hair, thin hair, or thick hair.

For help, look back at pages 6, 8, and 20.

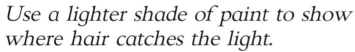

Use a lighter shade of paint to show where hair catches the light.

Showing noses

Noses are easier to paint from the side than from the front. Try painting the same nose both ways.

For help, look back at pages 12 and 14.

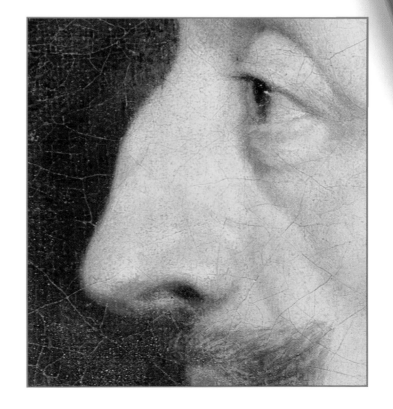

Face shapes

What shape is a face? Look through this book and look at people around you. How many different face shapes can you see?

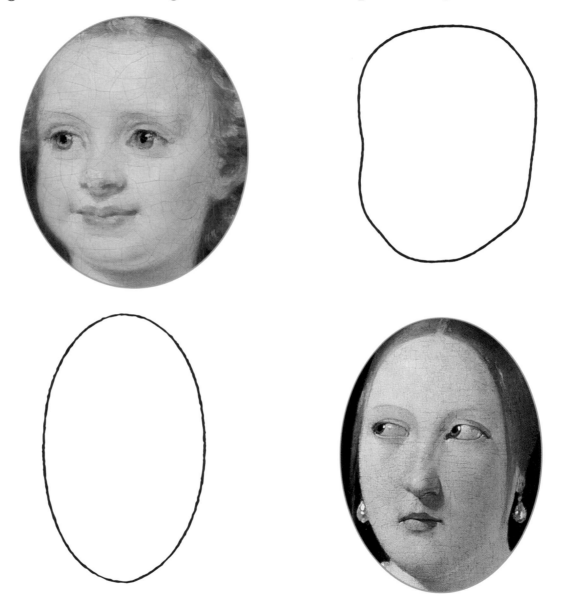

Try making a collection of face shapes. Draw the outline of each face and mark in the eyes and mouth.

For help, look back at pages 14 and 20.

Faces and feelings

Make a happy face, a sad face, or a surprised face in the mirror. Now paint your expression, choosing colors and shapes to match the feeling.

For help, look back at pages 16 and 24.

Turning heads

Faces can be painted from the front, the side, or anywhere in between. Try painting the same face from different angles.

For help, look back at page 12.

More about the paintings in this book

■ Portrait on a Roman Mummy *(page 4)*

The boy died in the first century A.D. His body was treated and wrapped in bandages to preserve it for the afterlife. His face was painted on a wooden panel, with colored wax, to decorate the head of the mummy and to keep his eyes open on the world.

■ Portrait of a Girl *(page 6)*

Domenico Ghirlandaio (about 1449-1494) set up a studio in Florence with his brothers and other painters. He was often asked to make paintings for wealthy people and churches. This portrait was made in his studio (in about 1490 judging by the hair style), but no one is certain who painted it, or who the girl was.

■ Johann the Steadfast and Johann Friedrich the Magnanimous *(page 8)*

Lucas Cranach (1472-1553) was a German painter. He painted this father-and-son portrait in 1509. Johann Steadfast was the Elector of Saxony. His son, Johann Friedrich, who was six in this painting, later succeeded his father as ruler. Typically, young Johann would have been painted with his mother, but she had died giving birth to him.

■ Summer *(page 10)*

Giuseppe Archimboldo (1527-1593) was Italian, but he worked at the royal court in Prague in what is now the Czech Republic. He created intriguing, entertaining pictures by constructing characters from plants and animals. *Summer* is one of four paintings representing the seasons. *Autumn*, *Winter*, and *Spring* also have heads created from fruits, vegetables, leaves, and bits of wood.

■ Triple Portrait of Cardinal Richelieu *(page 12)*

Philippe de Champaigne (1602-1674) was the best portrait painter of his time in France. The King's powerful minister, Cardinal Richelieu, asked him to paint this three-sided portrait. It was then sent to Rome to guide a sculptor who was working on a statue of the famous man. Champaigne even wrote helpfully above the face on the right that this was the best likeness.

◼ The Cheat with the Ace of Diamonds (*page 14*)

Georges de La Tour (1593-1652) was a French painter. He painted ordinary-looking scenes and filled them with hidden meanings, using dramatic lighting to add to the air of mystery. In this painting, the three on the left seem to be secretly in league against the young man on the right.

◼ The Young Schoolmistress (*page 16*)

Jean-Baptiste-Siméon Chardin (1699-1779) was a very successful painter of still life and everyday scenes. He loved painting children who were caught up in their own activities, such as spinning a top, blowing bubbles, or playing school. He wanted to show how they felt and thought as well as what they looked like.

◼ The Graham Children (*page 18*)

William Hogarth (1697-1764) was a British painter. He started as an engraver, and this painting was his first successful large-group portrait. Among the shining, smiling faces, the cat eyeing the bird is a reminder of death. In fact, the youngest child, Thomas, died before the portrait was completed.

◼ Self-Portrait in a Straw Hat (*page 20*)

Élisabeth Marie-Louise Vigée Le Brun (1755-1842) was witty, charming, and beautiful. She often painted the Queen of France and her children before the French Revolution. She took the pose for this self-portrait from *The Straw Hat*, a painting by Rubens that she especially admired.

◼ Doctor Paul Gachet (*page 22*)

Vincent van Gogh (1853-1890) was born in Holland and moved to France in 1886. He spent the last few months of his life at Auvers, painting every day. He often painted Dr. Paul Gachet, who looked after him there and became his good friend.

◼ Weeping Woman (*page 24*)

Pablo Picasso (1881-1973) was Spanish. In 1936, the Spanish Civil War broke out. In 1937, Picasso painted *Guernica* to show the suffering caused by the war. He continued to think about this sadness, and, in the next few months, he created a whole series of paintings of weeping women. This painting is the last in the series.

Glossary

expression: the showing of a feeling, thought, or emotion.

frame (v): to surround, as if in a frame.

gaze: to give a long look at; to watch.

glints: reflects a flash of light; gleams.

jagged: having a rough, uneven edge.

magnanimous: showing generosity and a noble spirit.

mummy: a person's body that was bandaged and preserved after death.

portrait: a picture of a person's head or sometimes the person's entire body.

self-portrait: a picture made by an artist of him- or herself.

shading: giving a degree of darkness.

startled: surprised.

steadfast: faithful; unmovable; firm in beliefs.

subject: an object or person that is talked about, thought about, studied, or portrayed.

Web Sites

KidzDraw
www.kidzdraw.com/artist.htm

Sanford Art Education
www.sanford-artedventures.com

Due to the dynamic nature of the Internet, some web sites stay current longer than others. To find additional web sites, use a reliable search engine with one or more of the following keywords: *art, William Hogarth, painting, Pablo Picasso, portraits,* and *Vincent van Gogh.*

Index